TEETH

TEETH

DALLAS HUNT

NIGHTWOOD EDITIONS

2024

Copyright © Dallas Hunt, 2024

1 2 3 4 5 — 28 27 26 25 24

ALL RIGHTS RESERVED. No part of this publication may be reproduced, stored in a retrieval system or transmitted, in any form or by any means, without prior permission of the publisher or, in the case of photocopying or other reprographic copying, a licence from Access Copyright, the Canadian Copyright Licensing Agency, www.accesscopyright.ca, info@accesscopyright.ca.

Nightwood Editions
P.O. Box 1779
Gibsons, BC VON 1V0
Canada
www.nightwoodeditions.com

COVER DESIGN: Angela Yen
COVER ART: Michelle Sound
TYPOGRAPHY: Rafael Chimicatti
INTERIOR ILLUSTRATIONS: Meghan Walley

Nightwood Editions acknowledges the support of the Canada Council for the Arts, the Government of Canada, and the Province of British Columbia through the BC Arts Council.

This book has been printed on 100% post-consumer recycled paper.

Printed and bound in Canada.

LIBRARY AND ARCHIVES CANADA CATALOGUING IN PUBLICATION

Title: Teeth / Dallas Hunt.
Names: Hunt, Dallas, author.
Description: Poems.
Identifiers: Canadiana (print) 20230592139 | Canadiana (ebook) 20230622798 | ISBN 9780889714526 (softcover) | ISBN 9780889714533 (EPUB)
Subjects: LCGFT: Poetry.
Classification: LCC PS8615.U676 T44 2024 | DDC C811/.6—dc23

for attie

CONTENTS

ankwacas 11
notes on grief 20
expel 21
crux 22
suplex 24
do you have any regrets! 26
axe 27
dim 28
meetings 29
what heaven 30
green k 32
dark tendrils 34
portraits 36
blunt teeth 37
there's a poem for everyone 38
shock 39
sound 40
169 "anomalies" 42
mâci- 44
maskosiy 46

how to make a galaxy 49
for miscanikwacas 50
bc ferries 52
wrinkles 54
my heart is fine, fine 56
the furnace 57
a deep swell 58
my kôhkom was a sentence 59
san solomon 60
a well 61
you can't kill a world 62
a sun after sleeping 63
blue whale witness 64

kaskitew maskwa 69
how i got home 73
orders to olive trees 74
westmount subjunctive 76
quills 78
i would nestle death 79
drowning in healing 80
floors 82
a yes cracks 83
no frontier (an ode to) 84
always going, to 85
dracaena 86
the wisdom of spiders 88
mason jars 90
scratch tickets 92
rant as review 93
slow and pause 94
cruel momentum 96
imperfect bodies 97
a carefully crafted spleen 98
a demand, for an atmosphere 99
there's a place between love and ruin! 100

glossary 103
acknowledgements 105
about the author 107

ANKWACAS

you can stream *alone*
now, on netflix,
a reality television
program that places
ten (voluntary) participants
in "harsh terrains" and
"inhospitable environments"—
sites that host the possibility

for intolerable bodily
pain, as well as
the psychic sting of
loneliness. for this,
for outlasting their
fellow competitors,
who are at a remove,
one will win $500,000,
the emotional
toll of being expunged
from the social

walking
down a crowded
street with a friend
towards the beach
of a west coast city
the day all luminosity
and cherry

blossoms, french
bulldogs and their
bulges, men
inexplicably shirtless—
no one, not even the sun,
asked for this

my friend notices
in the grass, exposed,
with one half
covered by shade,
the other side
simmering
in bare spotlight,
a dead squirrel

the ankwacas lies
with one appendage
reaching towards the
blades of
browning grass
with another
pressed neatly
against their side,
their body
the shape of a nap,
a comfortable
crescent
moon

nîtotem asks if
i would like to
stop and say
something, or
perhaps provide
an offering to
this deepsleeping
relative,
to which
i laugh
at the presumed
implication that,
because i am
cree, i will have
a prayer nested
in my pocket,

tobacco at the
ready, a remedy
or words to ward off
WD-40,
axle grease,
vegetable oil,
petroleum jelly,
commonplace weapons
used to intervene
and disrupt
the passages
of hungry ankwacasak
ascending bird feeder

poles in search of food,
small sustenance
for tiny bellies,
a remedy
to prevent tender feet
from slipping before
they flee for cover
i have none of this
in my lack,
in an invisible
apothecary bag,
in shame i ask
would ankwacas
do this for me?

in a "remote" area
just beyond the
greedy grips
of wildfires,
a contestant
on *alone* speaks
into a lens
without a
cameraperson
at the helm,
detailing his
hunger pains
and the bruising
emptiness of a
space without
others

the sole site
of camaraderie
is the base of a
tree, which houses
an ankwacas who
dutifully stands
at the edge
of a branch above,
each morning
chittering down
a welcoming bellow,
a gift to his solitary
compatriot below,
comrades in foraging

but with a growling
belly ringing,
ray, the contestant,
has to make an
impossible decision
between the weight
of existential
loneliness or
momentary reprieve
from the contractions
in his stomach,
between
abdominal aches,
fatigue, cramps,
the pangs of cravings
and doors closing,

friendship foregone,
a shaking, enduring
solitude

ray stops
referring to ankwacas
as his "little squirrel
friend,"
"a constant,"
"one like him,"
opting to use
"another food source,"
"game," "the
animal" and
"it's what's
for dinner" as
monikers instead—
an impending
death, both
literal and symbolic,
in referent

when a mojave
scissor snare
fails, ray proceeds
to retrieve
an arrow
from his quill
and hurl it
from a quivering
bow   to satiate

the maw of
his midsection,
and after he slays
ankwacas
ray confronts
the camera
and, in a showing
of masculine bravado,
states plainly,
"i was born a hunter.
let's face it"

but his expression
changes,
contorts, with
eyes seeking,
ducts plump,
small weeping,
at the demise of his
friend, ankwacas,
whimpering,
"i don't know why
i feel heartbroken
over this squirrel . . .
he treated me with an
uncommon familiarity.
and i betrayed his trust."
ray leaves
the show
shortly after

there are, proverbially, many ways
to skin a squirrel
to render their slight
fat to make anikwacâsimîciwin.
in urban fare
it looks like the
pin of a boot,
while gruff
hands, preferably
in gloves, relieve it
of its furry hide

or to be more specific:
cut the tailbone
from beneath,
turn the squirrel over
and step on the base
of its tail hold
the hind legs
in one hand and pull
steadily and slowly
until the skin has
worked itself over
the front legs and
head

after the incisions,
the pulling and
punishing grinding,
take half a cup

(or about four ounces)
of fat, and put
it in a six-quart
sauté pan
with approximately
two tablespoons of water
gradually cook
until it crisps
like overcooked
turkey bacon
let liquid evaporate and
pour the anikwacâsimîciwin
into a sealable plastic bag,
freeze

you will need a sharp knife
and no tobacco

NOTES ON GRIEF

for helen

grief is a house
painted matte black
to suck in the sun

grief is all the fixtures
of a condo wearing
to break at a moment's notice

grief is your kôhkom's hair
falling out because of chemotherapy
you a patient but failing hairdresser

grief is everyone
bickering and squalling
while trying to set things right

grief is a cineplex
wherein a house shushes, an open casket
a theatre into resentments of the living

grief is a gathering
that no one wanted to attend yet obligations
are the heaviest millstones to sink with

grief is a family
entangled, spiteful and yet declining
slowly together, like a sunset

EXPEL

you're not a bundle of mistakes. but do you remember when you thought
you knew what a spiral was? you're a place to crash
you spend your time sitting on life jacket bins on ferries and letting your
liver kill you. this world is too much for you, the enormity of it—how
can anything be this enormous? life is a bullet that finally gets there.
how do you outrun a bullet in open space

CRUX

an ocean means
so many things, it
lulls and hushes
it's a litter of
dreams, and
how they float;
fail—our dreams
so often
fail

oceans are beds
of rocks, abandoned
shells, crustaceous
families, dispersed
and destroyed, a
hull here, a bed to
lie in, to
build and leave
a wave,
a swallow

i rode a hope
across an ocean
once, and as the waves
lapped against the
sides, the boat
capsized and
tipped, and we
collided with the
reef, and
i think that's
the first time
i felt a dream
in real time—
splinters, and
blood
all at once

so often dreams
are desires
and broken teeth

SUPLEX

andré the giant,
a cousin
a relation
with a face
like a steam engine:
half doofus, half macarthur
grant fellowship

you and i:
two hearts
pulsating and
pumping over-
time to
mechanize
muscles
in a husk
that will
not live
past
forty-five years old

you were
never meant
to be a heel,
but commerce
makes heels
of us all

i hope
you're in a
vineyard somewhere,
with full belly,
sweat dripping
greenery chanting
your name—
sun beating and
you finally
small in the
face of all
things

DO YOU HAVE ANY REGRETS!

you ask me
to sing you
a song to sleep

i pick a song
i've forgotten
the lyrics to

but i sing
it anyway
and you humour

'cause love saves
and destroys us
all, the time

little snores
in flames
littler littler littler

a house made
from ashes, duct tape
and dust

AXE

he gives you ghosts
but a hotel room
is a forest
fire like when your dad
would flood the back rink
and then beat his wife

a body is a garden
of thistles, thorns and
failed attempts
but how good
to be engulfed
by the sun

sucklings in awe
as your body
topples—i don't
mind. i really don't.
i'll die someday

because an axe
makes kindling,
and what will
it make of
me

DIM

all books are warnings and yet the future!
the future! the future!

anger is a door and maybe that's not a bad
thing because it can open but

a stoop can be so lonely and tightly sealed
that you only glimmer next to the moths

who won't leave you alone and they stick
to the top of door frames. in truth

you're the visitor here. this sundering
sits with you, an occupied shared space

to love the light so much
you'd tear yourself in two

MEETINGS

the worst part is the wallow:
sweat-stained mattresses,
forgetting entire conversations;
things go "off the rails," it's not you
who dies, but the idea of you.
existing otherwise,
in the doing,
and hopefully, the being
undone (a fist unfurling).
the ditch doesn't have to be
about god—it's in the transference
and release. tenuous, fragile social
relation. all
wounded birds
same migration
patterns, same gathering
spaces. tenderly
held together

WHAT HEAVEN

spring, sapid
leaves,
a pallid face
on a warm
day

i am a boil that needs—
let me start
again:
a boil
that needs
lancing

a sense
of self
is a destructive
fiction—where
to go
from here

a group of
fictive selves
could be
revolutionary,
but maybe we
get lazy

a yearning for
the mess hall,
oriented around
affect, relations
bound by an
inarticulable trust

could be an ideal,
in the face of
heaven
and its
heavy fist

this poem should be
titled: "horizons
and their heavy fists"

GREEN K

everyone is
so small

inverted shells
cowering softly

dim lights
dank basements

frail yet somehow
blossoming

we make beds
out of moss

damp ground
sprouting quickly

tiny waves under
creaky branches

heads in
the sand

creepily, languid
ruin

every occasion
if you can

ruin ruin ruin
and the rain

will come
after

DARK TENDRILS

a scratchy throat
psoriasis for days
age like a suitcase
you've had since
you were twelve: worn out,
busted zippers
aches, unable to
let go,
a handle
barely holding
on

my hands
are leather
but not
comfortable—
they feel worn,
parched, that
someone else
got the better
out of them

not sure how
to say that
that someone
else was the sky—
i thought
perforation,
the way
out, a pinhole,
the size
of the
universe, but
the sky humours,
looms,
and that's
it—a greedy
mother to us
all

PORTRAITS

to be a waning sun
a riptide to be objects
that pull into the vast
calmly a family photo
a sunset on horseback
an edward curtis portrait, how
often the pull towards
death appears so
yearning and inviting like life is just
like that and we welcome it
too uncritically
i wish a waning sun would
implode that a riptide would pull
at us, gleefully
and that edward curtis would die
in the photo of his static lens,
and he was destined to live there
forever, cheap watches and all

BLUNT TEETH

we both have
off-coloured teeth
but there's a space
where plaque fails and
biology and chemistry
crumble

something else is born
there, i'm sure it looks like
desire, bark, old piano
keys, and yet the taste
is cold coffee that
feels like love

i'd feed you a thousand
mugs of aged caffeine
to live there, because
there are worlds in
bad breath, in
between our sticky
incisors and deep cavities

THERE'S A POEM FOR EVERYONE

i'm tired of indian poems. imagine a poem that wasn't about deer, moose or salmon. that we complained about how shitty the weather was, how a bush didn't offer the berries we wanted, how hard it can be to make a woven cedar-bark hat. i want a poem that doesn't tell how difficult something is because colonialism has made it so, but rather the elements, our relatives, being assholes and hard to work with. probably on purpose and intentionally so. a poem that sees us struggle with our kin because we fight with one another. and once this colonial edifice falls by the wayside we still have to grapple with the fact that some of our relations are difficult, but so are we, yet love is a tear duct that never closes, no matter how frustrated we are. do i have to be
_____?

just imagine! if you were outside the bounds of legibility, especially by literary communities. where you didn't have to write about trauma and moose meat and berries

SHOCK

for fred ottman, whom I know nothing about

speckled silver an announcement
a dirty floor a stage

everyone here is ridiculous yet
somehow you're viewed as the most

buffoonish of all and yet
something about you is abjectly

tender like you tried at something
your whole life and failed

but you tried and tried
now you coach little league

the shoddy drywall a guillotine
a safety manager but

you spill and spill and spill
and they laugh, bemoan, curse

but you rise above it all, do your spot,
and vanish. in a way true to your name

SOUND

wood dulls
and thuds,
a bow between
walls, yet it sings
if you listen,
like a môsom could,
or a kôhkom better

tentative marks and tracks left,
fresh heat coming off an imprint
the chase the most important
part, but gallops are orchestras too

a cacophony of hunger,
but you know your relatives
would do anything
for you, if it meant a full
tummy and a content smile

but your other kin
have something else
in mind, and they are quicker
than you are.
hopefully, you'll see
each other again, but neither of
you is entitled to that
anyway, rumbling stomachs
an invitation
but not an
entry pass

169 "ANOMALIES"

169 "anomalies" is a brutal
and brutalizing
way to end
a sentence

in the present
it asks how do
we hold space
in this world?

nuns used to break rulers
on my câpân's hands
while missionaries declared
"i can work
the weight of god
off you"

and then your
family members
sit in an unmarked grave:
the enormity of this
is hard to comprehend

my ancestors were not
anomalies. they were
children navigating a
world made too cruel
for them

a benevolent country
with 169 bodies
in one acre
with two acres
left to search

MÂCI-

my soft body is full
of ghosts, waiting

to be torn apart
by spindly fingers

of ancestors, by
those meaning well

yet somehow punitive
you wishing you could

have smudged better
somehow, but it's never

enough, their shadows
looming while you're just

trying to find solace
in harmful places

haunting is hard
on everyone

your kin working arduously
while you're just trying

to do the work
but the work kills

but especially if you
don't do it, a perverse

inversion of love
and demanding pressure

i guess all love
is a demanding pressure

in short i should
be doing better

and my ancestors
know that, pursed

lips moving, through
time and space

MASKOSIY

i wanted to feel long distance
a landscape like a braid
blades that cut like grass

i wanted to float above everyone
like an angry prairie sky
ten minutes of rain a gentle fist

i wanted to house geese;
water crushes when it runs,
flooding ruins a fence

i wanted you and the prairies
bouquet of wild roses and crude oil
the roundest part of a flat universe

i wanted teeth that were a map of the world
scaling an oil rig for a better view
a knot of entitlements and fierce love

i wanted the world
but got the prairies instead
an earth that spreads and spreads and spreads

HOW TO MAKE A GALAXY

i hear clamours of:
"how do we make this
a better world!?"
or i hope i do
but it's a whisper
in the arid heat
in suffocating humidity
in an air that punches

but what if we made
a galaxy between you and me
stars bearing down
caressingly but lonely, too
because that space
is so infinite
for something
so bright, so steadily
regulating orbits,
and the keen
eyes of small beings

FOR MISCANIKWACAS

wading or wallowing in alien blue chemically infused water to treat
the detritus we expunge and impugn, a doorway a welcome mat to a
hospice, alone, about to be pissed on all unknowingly

a friend from the north explains that the walk from cabin to outhouse
is brittle and treacherous, the path from entry to entry is littered with
bears, so the journey to relief is quick and finite—upon arrival await
unsuspecting gophers that don't know the necessary shame that will
visit them, and as splinters of light enter from aloft so too does warm
liquid shower them from above as though god had a running nose, the
clouds heave spit, a torrential downpour to a sputter, a malevolent
runny faucet, a comforting quilt both warm and musty: engulfing,
malodorous, different from the spindling estuaries the grizzly bears
are shuffling towards

gophers cry foul when they are pissed on in the dark. bewildered and
indignant, they emit what sounds like a human scream, a shriek that
cuts twilight and paradoxically does not alert the bears to the atrocity
they're, unbeknownst to them, implicated in—that they've helped to
engineer. not taciturn. have you ever had to so critically relieve yourself
that you'd outpace a carnivorous mammal to piss in the undeserving
face of a small rodent, ruin their night before they let existence slip
from tiny paws, tender humiliated fists shaking at a dimly lit hole god
made in the sky, a tentatively opened door a scythe, an unwitting grim
reaper letting go from above

commit this to paper not because it is funny, but because the shared precarity in that moment is three-fold: a swelling bladder, the search for sustenance, warm shelter a buoyant grave. narrative a cruel momentum but not a desire here, write about this because of this surplus, because it is an affect that lingers on but does not know why it lingers. it's funny, shameful and stupid in the face of things too large, not a tale of treacly attrition but a gesture to an atmosphere unnamed. not to laugh, but to do it, for the gophers

BC FERRIES

there are so many sad people
on the ferry the queen of alberni
is symptomatic of loneliness
and yet people travel great distances
and, at times, tumultuous waves,
to be lonely in equally beautiful spaces
with inviting wakes and canned speech
over outdated speakers
if you arrive early enough,
you get to see the crew engage
in hand gestures to alert each other
that patrons can be let off the ferry
—think here of the X they make
with their wrists. anxious and
anticipatory, shuffling feet
before the barrier rises
no one talks to each other
on the ferry a performative vessel
of loneliness floating and floating
out of the berth
the water will wash the navigation
the only time you enjoy yourself
is when you procure
a small cardboard
bowl of too much
vanilla fudge swirl
ice cream to gorge on
out of earshot, your friends

stand at the bow,
 a laughing family beside:
"oh god, look at that mess,"
 heads shaking, buoys bobbing,
"alone with all that ice cream"

WRINKLES

i just want to age
so i can find peace
when the SSRIs work
wrinkles a haven
dopamine stable

i think we're all
attempting to be kind
in a world that does not
have room for us

poetry saves, salves and is iterative
in terms of how it affirms
in tender ways
'cause i'm wrinkly now
corpse will be buried
in my home territories
and that approximates
closure somehow

but how can you miss
the land so much
when you've been
so far away from it
for so long and,
when you hear its
whistle through corvids,
it irritates

i want the prairies to
say "i love
that furrowed brow,
those creases,"
earnestly—
who else will?

MY HEART IS FINE, FINE

they say if you try to run
while attempting to detox you

risk heart
failure,

i ran today
ten kilometres to

jackie wilson's "lonely
teardrops," but did

you see the sun today?
mean-mugging geese

and a superfluous pool
near a perfectly fine

shoreline and you panting while

poison works itself through
your battered organs

your footsteps a palpitation
to an impending flatline

THE FURNACE

skin slides quickly
but the nestle is
where follicles collide
where we must
must must must

dew from sweaty
lilies that linger
wilted eucalyptus
punishing windowsills
it hurts to be nested

time stays
quiet when there
is so much and so
little to say about
exploding particles

outgrowth and rupture
butter teeth
a furnace is
in the lying
teeth are a verb
teeth teeth teeth

A DEEP SWELL

you realize late in life
that "there is no cure
for loneliness." and i tried
is never good
enough.
half measures a tablecloth glued.
everyday economies of care
a life raft.
harm reduction and horizons,
like a row
boat into a tidal wave.
everyone likes a
calamity in public,
and couch cushions kill
if you let them

MY KÔHKOM WAS A SENTENCE

curt but kind
grief will make a home out of me
a cave where ghosts dwell
i'm a home for ghouls
frankenstein's monster is my father
how much mileage can i get out
of these metaphors

grief is making up
excuses to go poo
at a party when you're
actually just trying
to steal away
to the bathroom
to cry

my kôhkom died today
grief a meteor
a muddy shed
a shovel full of piss
who knew there were so many
vessels for grief
i never saw her eat

SAN SOLOMON

strings are how it starts
rope is how they hogtie
farm animals
your relatives

drums are thunder
in these situations
a piano key a sliver
that won't leave
a crescendo is what they
call a cavalry
a horse regiment,
that beats with the bullet

san solomon is in texas and i won't
tell you the story of its settlement
what battles went on there
about the "saloons" or "shootouts"

and i won't tell you about
the first peoples there
their faces, their economies or
their families, but i do encourage
you to look it up, because
how informative would it be
to look up the communities
we plunder and
pummel

A WELL

every Indigenous person
east or westward
receives an email,
a request,
each one an arrow

my resting face
is a mute yawn
there's a harbour
somewhere
remember when
chaos was in orbit

how am i going to die:
my kidneys fail, they collapse
a branch an anvil
a river wraps its arms
around me

a fire's caress
an eager bus
a freefall, from anywhere
the dull of loneliness

who cares, really
i just want to know
what freedom feels like

YOU CAN'T KILL A WORLD

for jeanie

you didn't smile in
photographs. but none of
us did. i understand why

you were, in many
ways, the definition
of kinship. you
were life and light
and bright, and
we miss you

thank you
for mopping my
mother's floors,
for sitting around
for idle gossip,
for a warm
smile always

you were there
and now you're gone
words fail
never you

A SUN AFTER SLEEPING

what does it mean to die in the future
an unending skyline?
i brush my teeth upside down
to keep the plaque away
it surrenders and houses itself in my gums anyway
a skyline could be a way out
at least it recedes.
freedom with yellow teeth.
teeth fragments.
bustling openings,
it seems. particles dissipate.
waning leaves and the wilt,
in the face of a relentless sun.
the possibilities
of an unfinished painting.
i fell off a bridge
to nowhere.
no death is too small.
did you know brain cells reach
out for connections. they stretch
and stretch and stretch.
for immanent terrain.
with no hands to grab onto
sometimes. like galaxies.
but maybe, let's find our own suns
tender hands on a star

BLUE WHALE WITNESS

two under
covers, a shaky tipi,
built out of doomed love

there, always, stoking
fires and burning
under hot
coals. you wake up
saying a name,
and so maybe
this is what haunting
feels like

what absence is
rising each morning
to your own hoarse whisper
followed, in tow, by
a glottal stop

syllabics eroded and
forgotten. an absent
presence is
still an absence

knots cling to your bones
they're a black room
with a mattress
stationary, fetal
foam crib with
a musty pillow,
a ragged blanket

you find worlds
in people,
you find worlds
in a hug
without them

KASKITEW MASKWA

nohtâwiy works for
the resource extraction
industry, and handles
pumpjacks, water
lines, he caresses
the tools he needs
and the wheel
of the bobcat
he putters
around in

in his work
boots, underneath
a high wooden
pole, nohtâwiy begins
to climb, to labour
up the pole to
a platform

one that holds
him and his
breath hand in
hand, ascending
upwards toward
smoke and invisible
violence, toxins

until he notices
a black bear, mal-
nourished, teeth
missing, using its
paws, clambering
after him

nohtâwiy continues
to scale the wooden
beam, but maskwa
is relentless, aching,
doggedly scampering
up the pole
he is starving

the reason that wooden
beam and all
of its platforms exist
is to pillage the earth,
to destroy the hunting
grounds that the black
bear needs for nourishment
for itself and other maskwak

a contract broken
between those who
inhabit a shared space.
nohtâwiy decides
to jump
onto a pumpjack
and shatters
his leg in the process

he walks
with a cane now
and that bear, and nine
others, will be put
down, to find the
culprit in all of
this, to sniff out
DNA and emaciation

aside from the leg
nohtâwiy now suffers
from social anxiety,
like most of us do,
including kaskitew maskwa,
the black bear, who
witnessed a world
crumble around them

nohtâwiy is afraid of
public spaces now
malls, hotels and
familiar haunts that
have been full, to
the gills, since he was
a child

nohtâwiy is afraid now
as though each person
has a bear in them
waiting to come
out, desperate
and aching and,
maybe they do

HOW I GOT HOME

i grab the sun
and hurl it into your mouth
the brightest smile
i have ever seen
you catch and distribute
orbits, gravity fixing
that overbite you used
to worry about
to get through the silence
to get through bad nights
and i would ask,
who carries pîsim?
but it was you

ORDERS TO OLIVE TREES

arid olive trees in this
instance. a speech act at
the edge of the world
accompanying,
apocalyptic films
providing the genre of
interpretation, the
grammar through which
to view events, the
"logical" limits or ends to
"situations" such as
these. cries smothered
in open air, a vast
blackness an instagram

reel. seeing and hearing
things that cause your
joints to wither, your
spine to crook. a
catastrophe that is
exceptional and, history
reiterates, not
exceptional, simultaneously. an
analogue an ocean
away and we're both just
trying to embrace a river

to drink water without
impediments, to eat
freely in the company of
loved ones. a precedent
of dispossession,
displacement and
recontainment set by
benevolent white fingers,
tracing the
curvature of wrinkly
hands around a spoonful of soil

a history of the future
made by men with
dentures, wearing lapels
that communicate
sovereignty with an
open hand, not a quiet,
they insist, incessant
fist

WESTMOUNT SUBJUNCTIVE

when eyes burst
sight foreclosed
precluded horizons
when you're diagnosed
as losing your ability
to see at thirty-five

you don't care about
vistas or vast beaches
you worry about
the everyday
your favourite convenience
store, where you can
identify barbecue corn chips
wherein you recognize
the person who has
had you at checkout
since you've been here

service people do
more work than any of us
and you miss
the sight of them
the warming smile,
helpful hands, guiding
you to the
snacks they know
you want most

pay service
workers
more, since
without them
there are no
hands, nothing

appreciate the "unconditional"
kindness of those
who know what is
wrong, but do not shame
you for it. to those who
climb hills, even if the
terrain is different
you appreciate love
even if it lasts seven minutes,
an aisle tour
and the end result:
a bottle of gatorade
and tortilla chips.
to you, that is
what love looks like
in the face of
alienated labour:
a falling hill
but with arms on the
edge of it, inexplicably
waiting to catch you

QUILLS

for r.a.

i would hold your hand
anywhere, metallic or plastic
wishing to be
in there
with you, staring
at the end
of the world
together, and that
i could have walked
you over
trailing behind

i think about you
often—i think
about you,
and i want you to
know that.
i hope
that you
know that

I WOULD NESTLE DEATH

okay with being
a goodbye
like looking into a lung—
the sky bruises,
a calling crisis
as long as that
call is for me

i would nestle death
if it would stay away instead of me
sleeping with my mouth piqued,
in a silent scream,
paused
while it makes
its way

i would nestle death,
smother it with a hug
so the ones
i love have a chance without the grim
reapers and their
blades

DROWNING IN HEALING

night alone
a pebble
in your mouth
words for teeth
salty blank
tongues

it comforts you,
to be facedown
in the wayside.
why does treble
shatter

it's 1:26 a.m.
and we will
be broken open

how do you
hear me
always, how are you
everywhere,
mining and
pulling

glucose and thiamine
IVs that last
for days
make immobile
glued to a

bed with no sheet
for the mattress
i'm drowning
in healing

what pain comes from
swelling and sodium,
laboured breathing and
bruised toes,
needles and their
tiny pinches, fluids
flooding constantly

this is not the way
of our elders
but we make do
we make
use of the everyday
as it makes use
of us

sterile equipment that looks
outdated and new
all at once become
ligaments, ambivalent
creatures marking
respiratory patterns
and the tiny pleas
our hearts make
to stay alive

FLOORS

will chase
love, the
dark alley
ways and
open fields

chasing love is
our furthering
and so,
let it come
for you,

open to
a cartography
or open gate
to a portal,
partial but
a glimpse
to a new world

what a great
gift death
makes
for new worlds

A YES CRACKS

a composting in real time. metabolize, if you can. hogtied to a future
    not for many
a voice cracks the quiet limits of the world until no binds and no
    catacombs wait
for us and for use. burst through the ceiling and what could freedom
    look like

NO FRONTIER (AN ODE TO)

hammer grass plough klondike

day plough buffalo heat

hoe flies night grain

mosquito joy grief field

rich dry harvest fire

cow fly sign slither sugar

heat weed pavement jack-

hammer street heavy tires

grain field klondike day

ALWAYS GOING, TO

a wooden table
a gift
as an urban ndn,
furniture means a world, a life
without pity—imagine a life
without weight
even though your ancestors,
or cousins of your
ancestors, have
lived here forever
that the last gift they'd
give you would be
shame

DRACAENA

broken toenails, bone
broth for lunch, a smile

a chandelier, a balcony
a respite, where embarrassments

and conversations
flow freely

missing sadness
because it makes you

know what loss is.
yearning for planets

colliding, a horse
sinking in mud

a tipped-over
trashcan feeding

the earth, with metal
teeth the mother

of the world
pollution from

earth affects venus
an eleven-year-old

taught me that shortly
before kicking a soccer ball in my face

THE WISDOM OF SPIDERS

google maps:
counsellor's office —>
lions gate bridge —>
whole foods.
parhelia
maudlin, no longer

how nice it was to
see a snake eating
its own tail
harm comforting
coils, a braid
in miniature
grey hair
a skyline,
golden cascading
sun mistaken
for a moon.
trying to find

a buoy framed
the present,
the horizon
surrounding
an ill-hung
picture frame
teetering, precarious,

dipping so closely
toward a
hug from
lapping waves

MASON JARS

for maple

the sunrise and sunset
in my arms, gentle galaxies
ones who kick rocks and
fly down stairs

i miss love, no matter
where 'cause
love is matter,
a crafting
out of misery
shooting stars
are chipped teeth
who walk along
your feet, play
with kongs
and watch youtube
blankly, eyes akimbo

but you make
room for it
because how rare
is it to see
a shooting star?
the sun rise
and set at
the same time?
to see a galaxy emerge,
one that snugs
and loves
on their own
terms?

how lucky
to miss
people, to miss
the stars.
to cry after
supernovas who
just want
pumpkin purée
in the morning

SCRATCH TICKETS

the paradoxical safeguarding against loss produces loss. at least you don't "get hurt" in that you lose nothing—but how wonderful it is to fill that nothing and lose it sometimes!

shade in at the etches, edge an atmosphere, its margins a smudge, black marker on your palms and the sides of your fingers. etch-a-sketch a world and shake it to smithereens!

but a script is wearing a nice jacket to a restaurant and hating it the whole time, or the black shoes you have to wear even though they clomp too loudly against the sidewalk and you're self-conscious beneath its sound!

but then we have mussels at a restaurant that neither of us should be eating at and neither of us can afford, really, and everyone will judge our shoes and our obnoxious soles!

but i'll get to hold your hand and see an entire star fall behind you, the foreground: your face lighting up, ambient noise encasing. one of my shoelaces will be undone. we could be undone!

RANT AS REVIEW

it should adhere to the conventions of academic writing, or at least an ethics of filmic engagement should guide a superficial acknowledgement of Indigenous histories

light up marquees against big sky, an inexplicable cameo undercut a supposedly resurgent narrative, theatres of violence with buttery fingers, popcorn accompanying passive entanglements with history, recuperate the pioneers and fathers of cinema. reviews uttered into polite company and empty air, the blank space of colonialism against which traumas are rendered palatable or narrativized into pulpy interjections. a subjective camera view a lens into palatable suffering

a jarring and an opening ajar, carry the weight easy, where was joe pesci in red face when you needed him. weary writing and oblique critiques of pop culture, but what else is there to do when tantoo cardinal was criminally underused, when a film is bad and bad for you

SLOW AND PAUSE

amidst everything
weathered photo
an iphone taking a snapshot
of an ill-lit computer screen,
a photograph of a photograph
of a childhood home,
each mediation a lens,
an opportunity to fix, to
ossify, memory a slipping
pangea under the weight
of time, a manufacturer of
stress lines and creases,
of blissful and alarming
aporia, your haunts

haunt you, in the margins
an apparition mediating
a photograph, a picture
of a blurred house on a
bending crescent, the
street a wave of a hand

i hang photos on my fridge
of loved ones, with all of
their faces covered or
obscured, the hidden but
punishing sight of the ones
who love in spite
of

cherubs and
rogues leaping tight
from ledges
a home a castle
unexamined, but
thought of fondly

cat tails, bulrush
and weeds. brush waving near a plank
road that curves into
a residential area,
a sprawling orchard adjacent, with
berry trees and fruit bushes,
wild and cradled,
in the south
arm of the river

CRUEL MOMENTUM

what if i was a comet that fell to freedom what if freedom is a star plummeting providing light on the way down crops grow tan lines flourish and the sun descends quietly rush and pain but that's how stars vanish how lovely it would be to disappear bury me with my plants i hope a raincloud comes and undoes it all what is life but to feel like a speck sometimes love feels like finding another person to miss

IMPERFECT BODIES

more than a bundle of fists dirt in the pocket feet that wilt kilometres
    from hairline to

cuticle clogged pore pins that dot red enflamed lights and demarcates
    the way to intimacy

humble shuffle joints cold weather makes a creaking door shudder
    shut a dishwasher as a

trash can a kitchen island a drawer you thought you saw a bear hug
    a maw you step into

A CAREFULLY CRAFTED SPLEEN

to hide in, what difference
what worth—it doesn't matter

canada beckons, compiles
compels and makes certain
where you are with whom

still, the still of waters
under quaking, beneath
man-made earthquakes

the water we use to flush
a toilet is too much, but
to think of the water

in resource extraction projects
far exceeds anything
we could individually and yet

we feel guilty for letting,
for letting the water run
and don't gather to stop

these projects that use
far more water than we could
to imagine, to harm

A DEMAND, FOR AN ATMOSPHERE

cathexis: people have historically had a lot of shit thrown at them so it makes sense that they would appeal to the very institutions that enable the poor behaviour wielded against them to try to be granted something that resembles justice. if anything it points to the perversity of a societal structure and its attendant social relations, or the relations embedded therein, that they would appeal to the very system that operates through a mode of attritional violence (usually, but not always, but normatively, but) against them. petty sovereignty is its own straitjacket but that energy, that resentment has to go somewhere. it points to a felt intelligence that affect can be mobilized generatively, yet its trajectory, its means, are unknowable and

its ends are an atmosphere

the feeling of a wrong righted or its closest approximation. an appeal to a fault line for an earthquake. an avenue for release or deliverance that is still opaque or obtuse or, put crudely, does not exist in the world we have inherited. seeking momentary refuge in disinterested ears because attrition is fungible. and we are

all ambling toward an atmosphere

we would make better if we knew how *to make* better so instead we make do. fumbling is its own work. justice is a border, a boundary whose parameters expand and contract at varying times and to multiplying degrees. contingent and contextual, vacillation like a sound wave. an attempt to breathe polluted air in spite of its respiratory ailments

to insist on an atmosphere

THERE'S A PLACE BETWEEN LOVE AND RUIN!

i'm going to die either way, it's all about how i get there. i'm tired of myself. the thing about your heroes is they never save you, which should be a deep-seated contradiction, but it makes sense. and self-pity helps no one. people can smell a crisis. a crisis, at times, is not only how we're constituted, but it's "the very form in which we're driven out of the world." the hope is to find an ocean nested in shoulders—to reside there when the tidal waves come. and then love names the ruin

GLOSSARY

anikwacâsimîciwin squirrel grease
ankwacas squirrel
câpân a great-grandparent
kôhkom grandmother (translated literally means "your grandmother")
mâci- depending on context, can mean "wrong," "meanspirited" or even "evil"
kaskitew maskwa black bear
maskosiy a blade of grass
miscanikwacas gopher
môsom grandfather
nîtotem my friend
nohtâwiy my father
pîsim sun

ACKNOWLEDGEMENTS

"169 'anomalies'" was inspired by this story: David Opinko, "169 'anomalies' discovered at former residential school site in Northern Alberta," *Lethbridge News* (https://lethbridgenewsnow.com).

References in "ankwacas" are from the "About Squirrel" section of Rombauer's *Joy of Cooking*.

"there's a poem for everyone," "meetings" and "there's a place between love and ruin!" were originally published in *Contemporary Verse 2* (45.1) in summer 2022. "meetings" was previously published as "the ditch," and "there's a place between love and ruin!" makes reference to Saidiya Hartman after Michel Foucault.

"expel," "crux," "suplex," "do you have any regrets!" and "axe" were originally published in the *Capilano Review* (3.48) in fall 2022. "do you have any regrets!" was previously published as "expectation."

"the wisdom of spiders" takes its title from a reference to a reference: Lauren Berlant citing Sir Thomas Browne's *Religio Medici*. Note 19 of Berlant's *Cruel Optimism*.

kinanâskom'tinâwâw to everyone at nightwood editions for their diligence and hard work, especially janine, emma, karine and silas. kinanâskom'tinâwâw to all those i've written with or read alongside: cn, es, me, jj, bb, sn, sb, mcb, er, brb, kad, lh, rt, to, ss, ra, cn2, af, rvc, iw, tc, to name just a few. kinanâskom'tinâwâw to my family, here and beyond. big kinanâskom'tin to my cousin michelle for the cover art (https://www.michellesound.art/). kinanâskom'tinâwâw to my pups, atim and mapes. and kinanâskom'tin to you for your patience, too—you too.

Photo credit: Hollim Lei

ABOUT THE AUTHOR

Dallas Hunt is Cree and a member of Wapsewsipi (Swan River First Nation) in Treaty Eight territory in northern Alberta. He has had creative works published in *Prairie Fire, PRISM international* and *Arc Poetry*. His first children's book, *Awâsis and the World-famous Bannock*, was published through Highwater Press in 2018, and was nominated for several awards. His first poetry collection, *Creeland*, published in 2022, was nominated for the George Ryga Award for Social Awareness in Literature, the Gerald Lampert Memorial Award and the Indigenous Voices Award.